D0210066

A Bestiary
An Animal Alphabet

Poems by Richard Bonfield

Thankyou for helping to issue The beautiful Alphabet

A celebration

Richard Bonfield

Norwich
A Fine City
15 of 1993

COYPU PUBLICATIONS

First published in 1993 by Coypu Publications, 105 Portland Street, Norwich, with the help of the Ark Wrights.

A CIP record for this publication is available from the British Library.

ISBN 0 9521016 0 2

Printed in East Anglia by
The Modern Press, Bethel Street, Norwich, on acid-free, recycled paper.

Typeset in Adobe Garamond, titles in Futura Condensed.

CONTENTS

FOREWORD

"Smash open the Book of Time
And Archaeopteryx is dancing."

With *A Bestiary* you can dance with archaeopteryx. Or, if you don't fancy dancing, you can play with the dolphins, slither among the eels, embrace clankingly amidst the horseshoe crabs, bounce with the impala or even munch away at the Everglades with the manatees.

Richard Bonfield has "taken the great horn of an ammonite and blown an Ordovician blast" to invite creatures rare, strange and endangered to a celebration of species. From all around the planet they have answered his summons, and have been created anew by the synthesizing power of Richard's fantastic imagination.

This fantastic, often fun-loving imagination, coupled with an active concern for the plight of our Earth and its multitudinous life-forms, has produced that rare beast, a New Voice in Poetry. Since the day, more than two years back, when as Editor of *Poetry Nottingham* I first sighted a Bonfield poem, I have eagerly watched the progress to first collection, the hunt for a publisher, and the final decision to sod 'em all and go it alone.

Now that's enough Foreword – buy the Ark (25% of net profits goes to The Save The Indian Elephant Campaign), read the poems, enjoy the tingle factor and join the penguins in Hitting Top C!

Claire Piggott

Big Poem Hunter

The poet is trying to catch an animal
Silently he goes downwind
Armed only with a bag of metaphors
A roll of alliteration
Some flash bulbs of onomatopoeia.

Now he loads the camera with unpredictable imagination
Takes aim
And fires a volley of sunlit words

Usually the animal gets away
But sometimes
Only sometimes
He processes the film
And finds the creature
Fixed in the developing tray
In beautiful, lyrical focus

Dressed in the poet's distinctive colours

INTRODUCTION

This collection grew, initially from a seed bed of three or four poems. There was a moment when I wanted to shout "Eureka!" This was the day, over two years ago, when, prompted by Claire Piggott's suggestion that I should complete an animal alphabet, the words 'A Bestiary' suddenly shunted across the empty page of an even emptier mind. So, I had the title – obscure though it seemed, even to me. But the ark was almost empty.

Thankfully, after four years of imaginative herding, I have a full (if idiosyncratic) cargo. And this, I feel, is how it should be. The mediaeval bestiaries were full of fantastical creatures we now know do not exist. But fact is always stranger than fiction. It was only a few hundred years ago that we lost the Moa – an extinction brought about by the hands of the so-called noble savage. It was a startling revelation to me that some of the peoples we naïvely admire for their apparent ability to live in harmony with nature have, on the contrary, been the perpetrators of quite awesome extinctions of native species. Man has always been man. We've always had an eye on the main chance. But man is now a global animal, with (hopefully) a global vision and global responsibilities. Some along the way have learned that harmony is the best policy. We with our global vision must be made to see that harmony is now the *only* policy, both to preserve genetic diversity, our sense of wonder, and, ultimately, ourselves.

To all intents and purposes we are alone in the universe. Alone, that is, apart from the thousands of species which inhabit our planet, feed us, clothe us, and allow us to reflect upon ourselves. Man is only man. Live or die, the world will undoubtedly go on without us. We are the stewards of the planet, but we may not be the stewards of its future. However, we, at least, have the foresight to envisage our demise *and* to do something about it.

It's up to us to build the ark and rescue the beautiful alphabet. Everyone is Noah now.

Richard Bonfield
Norwich, March 1993

ACKNOWLEDGEMENTS

Some of these poems have previously appeared in *Poetry Nottingham, Z.L.R, Peace News, First Time, Foolscap, Green Voice* and *The Country Standard*
The poem 'Kingfisher' is soon to be published in *Outposts*

Excerpts from the collection were first read by the poet when he supported Heathcote Williams for his first public recital of 'Autogeddon' in St. George's Church, Colegate, Norwich in 1991. Proceeds from this event were donated to Greenpeace.

These poems and others from this collection were subsequently read by Judith Pearson and the author on March 24th 1993 at the Little Theatre, Leicester. The event succeeded in generating the remaining capital necessary to launch the ark.

Poems in this collection have also been reprinted by *The Country Standard* and the *Norfolk Friends of the Earth Newsletter*. Poems not included in the present collection have been published in *Envoi, Poetry Nottingham, Foolscap, The Frogmore Papers, Peace News* and *The Haiku Quarterly*.

Many thanks must be extended to Rupert Eris for deciding to use the poem 'Elephant' (with the last word altered to India) as a poster in a briefing pack to be given to all workers involved in the Save The Indian Elephant Campaign. I am very pleased to be involved in this project and to give a portion of the proceeds from the sale of this collection to such a worthy cause. (Information about the campaign's activities can be found at the back of the collection).

The illustrations throughout this collection are taken in the main from: *Winners in Life's Race* by Arabella Buckley; *Knight's Pictorial Museum of Animated Nature* and *Oliver Goldsmith's Animated Nature*. Posthumous thanks to their respective Victorian illustrators.

Ark Wrights

Listed below are all those who, by donating money, time and/or skills, have helped to build the ark:

Josephine Austin, Richard Austin, and family, Art Bailey, Kevin Bailey, Willy Bailey, Nick Barton, Sarah Bayliss, Bruce Bentley, Judi Benson, Ruth Berridge, Lou Betts, Malcolm Bolton, the Bonfield family, Ruth Bowden, Peter Brown, Kingsley Canham, Steve Caplin, Tom Carver, Paul Cheetham, Steve Clary, Pamela and Richard Clark, Sara Clark, Martin Cook, Neil Cross, Jai Deva, Paul Davies, John Downes, Jeremy Dunn, Bilbo Dunion, Andrew Elsegood, Rupert Eris, Wendy Gaston, Nick George, Maria Geurten, Stephen Goaley, N D Harrington, Cherry Hatch, Judith Havens, Carol Homden, Becky Horn, David and Jane Horne, Lesley Hunt, Babs Hurley, Roland John, Nick Kilenyi, Paul Large, Pat Laslett, Margaret Lewry, Robby Lewry, Cressida Lindsay, Marilda Macmaster, John O'Malley, Wolf Malucha, Kevin McCafferty, John and Maggie Midgley, Minka Nicholson, John Moore, Nik Morgan, Kathy Page, Roz Painter, Judith Pearson, Liz Pearson, Claire Piggott, Rosemary Raynor, Mike Riddle, Alan Scrase, Andrea Slater, Keith Smith, Heather Stallwood, Nick Stone, Roy Taylor, Joan Tuckley, David Waldron, Beryl Whadcock, Dr Peter Wilson and Eric and Marie Wright.

Special thanks to Mum and Dad. Thanks also to Lucas at Sunrise Studios; Password Publishing; Graphics Matter Ltd.; the B.F.G.; all at Peace News; Tigger, Sylvia, Frankie and all at The Green House; Peter Crowe, Antiquarian Bookseller.

And last, but by no means least, Paddy the cat (who, as usual, did nothing at all).

I made it, with a little help from my friends.

*To everything in Noah's Ark
and everyone who helped me build mine.*

Graphic Origination and Cover Design	*Martin Cook*
Animal Alphabet Calligraphy	*Art Bailey*
Text Editing and Page Layout	*John Moore*
Photography	*Jeremy Dunn*
Original Dolphin Illustration	*Steve Clary*
Axe Grip	*Bilbo Dunion*
Best Cat	*Paddy*

Thanks to ARTMART et al.

Thanks also to Claire Piggott, Judith Pearson, my family and other animals.
Not forgetting David Attenborough, Johnny Morris, Ted Hughes, Hans Hass,
Jacques Cousteau, Heathcote Williams and Charles Darwin, without whose
collective inspiration none of this might ever have evolved.

*Hand Made in Norwich
A Fine City*

Archaeopteryx

Smash open the Book of Time
And Archaeopteryx is dancing
Throwing out limbs of feathered limestone
Printed by lithographic silts
It is flying across the pediment of history
Pressed like a stone flower
A jigsaw of tempered porcelain
It is an Elgin Marble
A Magellan of air
Daedalus by Da Vinci
A Harpy floating on a vase of sculptured clouds.

Bats

Matchbox night monsters
Bats shave past you
Antennae bristling
Painting the swerving landscape
In brushes of shadowy noise
For inside their valve crammed heads
Night is lit by ultrasound
As they tune into the evening
To feed on radio dragonflies
That flicker across their wave bands

Like angels dressed in echoes.

Polar Bear

Calved from glaciers
Suckled on snow
Icicle coated
Down below
Waits for seals with Inuit poise
Breathing Buddhas make no noise

Kills so quickly, nothing's missed
Herring gulls devour the bits

Pads across the northern sky
Borealis in its eye

Climbs into its cave of stars

Sleeps till Springtime melts the bars

The Poet and the Blackbird

My gold nibbed pen
And this famished Blackbird
Both scratching a living
On Winter's empty page.

Bird's Nest Soup

High in the caves of Sumatra
Live the soup dragons' aerial friends
Birds whose flavoursome mucus
Is garnered for glutinous ends

The Passing of The Buffalo

The Buffalo are melting ice Bison
Fog Wildebeest
Once they swarmed on the Western plains
Like deafening shag pile
Once Indians made a culture and a civilisation from their
Tidal beauty
They clothed themselves in thunder
They fished with thunder
They carried their children in thunder cribs
They made love under heaving thunder leather
They painted these Coal Gods on their Rosetta breasts
They decorated their lives with their reason for living
But then the White Man came
And shot the Buffalo from trains
To process them into meaninglessness

And the Buffalo left the plains like weeping smoke
And there was no more thunder
And there was no more love-making
And there were no more children

And there was no reason for living.

Butterfly

In its occluded test tube
The spotty caterpillar
Is dissolving
Into caterpillar soup
To re-emerge
Between drying fans
Like a shy Geisha
Fresh from insect finishing school.

Two Butterflies

"Each year"
The man said to the child,
"My wife comes back as a butterfly.
On the anniversary of her death
She flies through our bedroom window
And hangs like a silk shawl over my frozen memories".

The man has long since died
Years have passed by
But, I often wonder if
On the anniversary of her passing
Two Admirals flutter gently through that melting window.

Chamæleon

The Chamæleon
Has more colour channels than Cable TV.
A brilliant interference in the tropical trees
It changes hue in the blink of an eye
From BBC1 to Boxing on Sky
It moves more slowly than a cheque in the post
But its swivelling sockets are its proudest boast
Revolving independent through the arc of degrees
Like Jodrell Bank on LSD.
As it swings around in the prehensile trees
Till the sockets engage on a plumptious moth
Which its tongue envelops in a spume of froth
Telescoping back into its horny head
End of transmission
And time for bed.

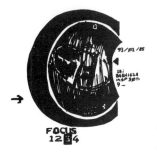

Christened by Four Rivers
(For Catriona)

Carried abroad in the soft skin suitcase
An English child is growing
In an ice-bound Canadian city

Born it will be showered with
rose petals and maple leaves
A confetti of cultures will attend its Summer birth
And its font will be carved by an Italian
Out of garlic flavoured marble
In a warm Florentian church.
It will grow up by the Saint Lawrence
With the ancient Thames in its veins
And, on the day of its worldly immersion
It will be bawling; gently occluded
By the sibilant tides of the Seine.

Coelacanth

A living fossil
He swims out of the rock

In four dimensions

His ancestors were, long ago
Embroidered in stone
But, he swims out of the rock
Today
A rehydrated horror
In antediluvian armoured bone

Meanwhile, in Loch Ness there are ripples

Well, the past is not always dead and buried

Ripples are not always caused by sinking stones.

Cuckoo Chick

April's town crier
The Feathered Pretender has just broken out of Wormwood Scrubs
Into a blue tit's chintzy lounge

The blue tits have been proudly sitting on him for weeks
Perched like houseflies on a stranded whale

He glares around
Like an African Frankenstein

Eyes up the scrawny competition

Welcome to the world, son, say his puffed-up parents
So glad to see you're vast and sound
These will be your brothers and sisters

Yeah, but not for long, thinks the brawny Cuckoo Chick
Leering at his ovular 'kith'

Soon to be king of the castle
As he proudly flexes his egg-flecked biceps

Greedily wolfing his first bowl of insects

Furtively eyeing the yolk-splattered ground.

The Fiddler Crab

The Fiddler Crab has eyes on stalks
And a claw so large it can hardly walk
It lives amongst the mangrove swamps
Where the David Attenborough yomps
And can often be seen at evening's end
Serenading its mud-skipping friends

With a Cajun Stradivarius.

Dolphins

Honed by Time's wind tunnel they
Groove down the barrel of a wave
Smiling blue beauty
The sea's best intelligence
Their home is the curving World
The sky the mirror of their singing spirits
And they are our friends if we choose not to
Crush their marvellous coral brains
These playful argonauts of shimmering peace
These beautiful arching brushstrokes in the
Garden of the ocean.

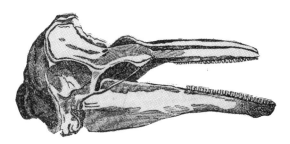

Spring on the Line
'A Nursery Rhyme'

Deep down
under snoring oaks
The dormouse is coiled in its thistledown cloak
With its tail at a quarter to Christmas
Its ears at half past Autumn
And its thoughts in the kingdom of disembowelled stoats

Up above
In the kingdom of the polar bear
It's been an unrelenting Winter

But listen now
And follow me down
For deep inside a sundialled lair
There's an answerphone message from the Mad March Hare

And underneath the waking oaks

A million flowers are clearing their throats.

Eels

Eels are silver moon spawn
　　Sargasso spaghetti
Torques of twisting mercury

Eels are field slitherers
　　Necklaces of night
Cleopatra's chromium cousins

They are born on the night of mulch
Transmuted from mulch
Translated into twisting Talmudic script
They write themselves across the evening weather
To the music of Cassiopeia's harp
These quivering compass needles
Follow the scent of the underground sun
To the Rome of all eels
Ariadne's ball
The Astrolabe of Eeldom
Turning like Medusa's hair

In a merry-go-round of flailing light.

Elephant

The great Earth Whale
With its curves of pearl
Is a swirl of grey on the cusp of the morning
A brethren of blended shadow
A glorious mass of heaving heaven

Lonely on the rim of the World
Calling to the Planet
To save itself from idle pleasures

The lathe-tooled trinket
The hand-carved toy
The smiling Buddha's
Carved jowls of joy

But soon the Elephant itself
Sculpted from its own sacrifice
Hacked from its own bones
Will stride the mantlepieces of suburban homes
Forever mute to the ivory music of midnight guns

Quiet as the sun-bleached skulls
That litter the mantlepiece of Africa.

Galapagos Finches

Similar Finches with different beaks
Gave Darwin pause for sea-sick weeks
As he retched in his cabin
And pondered nightly
Over common birds
With different tools
For nicking nectar from flowery hooves
Some with nutcrackers
Some with spoons
Some with chisels
And some with brooms
Each of them evolved to fit the bill
Of the empty niche they had flown to fill.

Angler Fish

A deep sea dong
With a luminous nose
More surreal than Lear could compose
The angler fish has its own porch light
To welcome guests in the dead of night.
The light says there's bed and board to be had
But the teeth say there's nothing but the butchers slab
As this *comely* moll with the alluring fag
Cruises like a bacon slicer dressed in drag.

Fossils

I took the great horn of an Ammonite
And blew an Ordovician blast
In memory of the fossilised past
And all along the railway cutting
There were wheels and trumpets
Belemnites and Plankton saxophones
An orchestra of compressed stone
A fugue of rich Cretaceous bones
A graveyard of an ancient sea
An awesome armoured symphony of
Creatures moulded in marlish tears

Lying quietly under Leicestershire.

THE ANCIENT FISH & THEIR HUGE RIVAL

Fox on The Grand Union

Look!

Slipping between Winter reeds
A Fox on this Christmas canal
Ice sandalled
Padding on Winter water

A fox on this Christmas canal
Snow slippered
Prancing on smoke and Guinness

A Fox on this Christmas canal
Tip-toeing
Tap-dancing on crunching leaves

A Fox on this Christmas canal
Magically fox-trotting
Across Winter's frozen eaves

Taking one last glance for danger

Before slipping between evening trees.

Giraffe

Warily he drinks in camouflaged communion
Arching the neck with its seven bones
He prays to the gunpowder river

Curtseying his quilted hide
Defenceless in his clumsy elegance
Like a Samurai without his sword
He swings
Beautifully low
To sip Kilimanjaro's melted snows

Lamarck's living ladder
He browses in the higher reaches
A question mark on the rolling plains
He glooms like a gentle watch-tower
Engulfed in thundering Wildebeest flames

A sentry of the Serengeti
He watches over Africa's darkening ocean
Like a leather staircase to the sunrise hours

Like a living, breathing

Periscope of flowers.

Gorillas or Guerrillas

Once upon a myth
When I was much younger, and much less
hirsute than I am now
I finally came face to kneecap with
The Ghastly Gorilla in my local museum

Now, I'd seen specimens of him in the local pub
He was a skyscraper of moth-eaten savagery
An equatorial Troll
Wildly brandishing a brain-smashing club
Killed, in the nick of time by a
'Noble' Victorian hunter of
Unquestionably bluer evolutionary blood.

For a long time after that I thought that
Gorillas were Guerrillas
For a long time after that I thought that Fidel Castro was a
Wild
Cigar puffing ape
Who used Malibu aftershave
And ruled a place called Cuba
With an iron banana
In a velvet glove.

It was only later I realised that Gorillas were not
Guerrillas
It was only after David Attenborough I realised that,
After dying of gout in the Gentleman's Club,
It was the 'noble' Victorian hunter who should have been…

...STUFFED

And mothballed in the museum of mankind's savage ways
To teach errant gorilla schoolchildren a salutary lesson

On rainy days.

Hedgehog

Autumn's pincushion
The lovely moonpig
Is
Teasingly
carelessly
Studded
With dead September leaves
As she shuffles down the catwalk
In an off-the-hedgerow number
Her body liberally sequinned
With hundreds of glittering fleas.

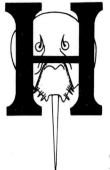

Horseshoe Crabs

On the strangest night of the year
When the moon is as full as a crab in love
They swarm the unspoken beach

This is D-Day for the grey dinner plates

Seething in the ocean like a soup of armour
The Moon Trilobites
Emerge from our Cambrian nightmares
And let down their fossilised hair
For a night of frying pan love.

On the strangest night of the year
When the moon is as full as a crab in love
The Horseshoe Crabs remember that there must be
More Horseshoe crabs
Then the moon unlocks their stone libidos
And they clankingly embrace
                    Beneath the crab above
Massing like drunken Daleks
To spoon with their dustbin lid doves.

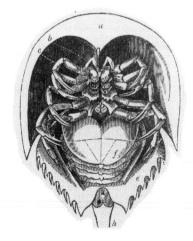

Impala

Bouncing on African springs
The Impala is impelled by the golden scent of death
To float away from slouching danger
In blazing fawn parabolas.

A North American Indian Explains Systems Theory

Know that the land is a web and a flow
Know that nothing is greater
Man is of a piece with the Beaver, the Elk and the Cedar
In felling the Cedar a seed is planted
In killing the Elk prayers are offered
In killing the Beaver room and time is left for others to grow

In the land of web and flow man treads the path
And leaves no trace
Neither high nor low man is himself the ebb and flow
Through the flowing land ebbs the hunter
Through the web of the spider the seasons come and go

No webs are broken here
In the forest the flowing hunter follows the Tao

And everything rejoices in relation.

The Jackdaw

One of Fagin's spivvier boys
The Jackdaw is a feathered kleptomaniac
From the roofscapes of the Gorbals
Over-fond of other people's private joys
Sentimental baubles and Cartier toys
But it has no sense of aesthetic taste
So that diamonds end up in the household waste
It just enjoys collecting for collecting's sake
To feather its East End nest
In the very worst of eclectic haste
So that Miros end up with Weeping Girls
And Woolworths rubs shoulders with Fabergé pearls.

The Kingfisher

The Kingfisher
Erupts from charcoal
Like a Zen painting
Touched to colourchrome life
It has gathered the stray shades of Summer
Into a loom of Chinese lightning

Caught in the rood of trees
Like stained glass viewed from a spartan season
It roosts underneath the leaking chapel of Summer

Flies
Like a water-colour fireball on a smoky Autumn evening
Like a splinter of Nirvana in the gentle English snow.

Lamb

A present posted in yesterday's Summer
Autumn's gift to the year beyond
A cumulus loaf from a snow-swept oven
On the uplands of expectant Derbyshire
The Herdwick is licking a bleating rose
As Spring unwraps its gift to itself

Snow Leopard

A dappled Koan
Enlightenment's smoking shadow
The Snow Leopard rustles prayer bells
Yaks move uneasily
The moon looks on
But the Snow Leopard can only be felt
By its prowling absence
Slipping softly over the mountain passes
Leaving a kill to the frost feathered vultures
It explains itself by drifting enigmas
Always one leap ahead
It is a snow shaman

Looking at you
Looking for it

Just beyond your engulfing lens
A paw-print filling with Autumn prayers.

Literary Lion

The Lion is a hive of yawning honey
Lazy brother to its sister star
It lions in the welcoming trees
Like a badly padded pyjama bag
Its tongue lolling like a felt heart
Its tail dangling like the silk tassels
Of Noel Coward's velvet bathrobe.

The Manatee

The Manatee is the sailor's ugly mermaid
The sea's fishy doughball
The cow that swims on water wings
Munching the salad dressing of the Everglades

The Manatee is the seal's ugly sister
The blubbery girl that never gets to dance with the
Double breasted Dolphins

Weeping under the water hyacinths
She is always looking for Cinderella's slipper
To fit her ugly flipper

She is always looking for her contact lenses
In the salty washing up.

The Praying Mantis

The Praying Mantis is part Heath Robinson
Part Edgar Allen Poe
It is all paper clips and Jaws
An Origami Dragon
Ralph Steadman's Spidergraph of Satan
It is all green levers
And Gossamer saws
It is all Vincent Price
And revolving doors
And Sweeney Todd is living in the apple of its eye
And Norman Bates is Mother in its window in the sky
Where the Praying Mantis crunches on a struggling Butterfly
And leafs through its chitinous Bible of atrocious ways to die.

N

Narwhal

The Narwhal is an ivory corkscrew
Opening millions of gallons of
Arctic Beaujolais.

Ostriches

Mata Haris on drumstick legs
With beautiful lashes
And boxing glove feet
Ostriches carry their beautiful tresses
Bouncing above the can-canning heat
Baring their thighs for all to see
Plenty of African flightless meat
Plenty of flounces and plenty of curves
And beautiful plush on their moulin rouge seats

Owl

To the Owl night is an infrared banquet
Beyond its suddenly unlidded eyes
The frosted windmill is a velvet boneyard.

Two great plates of light
An undercarriage of intricate butchery
And a beak for tearing the hearts from hares
The Owl is prowling across its demesne

Dreaming from the barn
It is gliding to harvest its tithe of velvet

Later
Far down
Far down below
Like a moth drawn irrevocably to the light of life
A leveret is smelt in the infrared
Warm blooded in the hooting nightfinder
Then, the pendulum descends in swathes of silence

Two great plates of night
An undercarriage of intricate butchery

And the dawn is bleeding
And the grass is screaming.

Oyster

The Oyster is an unwilling jeweller
Who uses an alchemist's gland
To spin soothing Fabergé worlds
Round aching grains of sand.

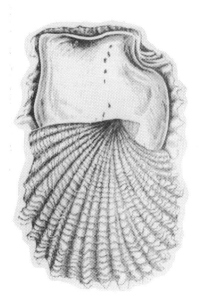

P

A Panda Gives The Reith Lectures

The Panda has taken off his spectacles
He is rather hot and flustered
He is giving The Reith Lectures on endangered species

He drinks a glass of bamboo juice
Shuffles his papers.

Gosh, isn't he cute, says a pubescent white rhino
In an ill-fitting, double-breasted
Mike Tyson sort of suit

I wish he'd been around when I was here, says a ghostly Quagga
I hope he'll put in a hoof note for me?

I'm sure he will, dear, says a kindly giraffe
Who has temporarily entangled her earrings in the lighting rig.
Meanwhile lion bars rustle, warthogs sneeze, wildebeest bellow
An owl begins to hoot

Ahem, says The Panda
Glowering benignly

I would like to begin, says The Panda
Replacing his spectacles
By reading a paper on our *most* endangered species

Well, the necks all turn
Searching for this marvellous, cuddly creation
This wonder of the world
This great, endearing brute

But, to the consternation of The Panda,
The human has already left

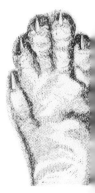

With the animals in pursuit.

Penguins

Penguins enjoy listening to the music of waltzing icebergs
Penguins enjoy balancing their Penguiny eggs on their yellowy legs
Penguins enjoy standing under the Albert Hall of the
Aurora Borealis
Watching Orion conduct the Penguin Suite

Penguins enjoy milling around
Penguins enjoy Snow Operas and Ice Cream Sodas
Penguins enjoy sliding about on their bottoms
Like brakeless Skodas
But most of all Penguins like to
Fly underwater

Free falling off the ice cliffs like newspaper lemmings
They open their stubby throttles
Like formerly sedate, opera-going Flemings
And roar into Swanhood
Blasting off into the icicled Antarctic
Hitting Top C
Leaving a lot of surprised people with empty wrappers
Feeling deeply embarrassed that they'd made fun of these
Blubbery, snow vested Pavarottis
These black and white chocolaty flappers

That were meant for their afternoon tea.

P

Plankton

It all comes down to Plankton in the end
Gazpacho for Whales
Snow monsters in a Victorian lantern.

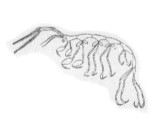

The Quagga

The Vultures are congregating around the last Quagga
Like a convention of feathered Professors
Debating a dead language
With massively wattled jowls
They are sad that such a moth-eaten 'Zebrass'
Should have thrown in the four-legged towel.
But, they are oddly happy to eat it
Like a brood of College fellows locked in
Gormenghast's Stygian bowels
Denuding the sweltering carcass of an
Overdone Christmas fowl.

53

Manta Ray

Long before Star Wars and stealth bombers
I was tucked up in bed with the autobiography of Hans Hass
Diving to adventure with the Manta Ray
This was the close encounter *I* dreamed of
There was nothing more alien than this,
Nothing more awesome than the vast
Undulations of Neptune's outrider
It was the deep's atavistic Pterodactyl
Part of the Nazgul's submarine contingent
And I was its secret pilot
Coming in low over the coral
On the supple diamond
Black as Mecca
To drop the fires of my imagination

On a sea floor lit by a bedside light.

The Reindeer

The Reindeer are listening with their coat-hanger heads
To Radio Chernobyl
They have picked up something
Smelt the rotting atoms in the wind
And the Lapps are watching the Reindeer

Kneeling in their Reindeer coats
They explore the look of puzzlement
The genuine fear of invisible invasion
The Red Army of radiation which is
Seeping into their Christmas culture

No, Father Christmas will not be flying this year
For the Reindeer are mutating
In Reindeer wombs throughout the land
Reindeer are being born
Without the power of flight.

On Christmas Eve children will be waiting in their hospital beds
But their souls will not be filled
And their hair will continue to fall like snow
And the Reindeer will continue not to come
And there will be no presents
And there will be no laughter
And the snow will fall like a cloud of skulls.
Mothers will leave out sherry and mince pies
Vodka, snow cakes and warm hay

But their children's hair will continue to fall like snow
And there will be no presents
And there will be no laughter
And the snow will fall like a cloud of skulls

And the Reindeer will continue not to come.

Haiku for a Robin

In my emptied garden
This glass of Autumn wine
Brims on Winter's table

Great White

A sunken longship
Jaws wide as unsated Grendel
It scours the sea's underbelly
Smelling the ocean's palpable fear
Closing in on terrible weakness

A gilled psychopath
With clanking rows of eternal teeth
It powers from pole to pole
An ever-moving abattoir
Perfect in its primitiveness

A scarred Nautilus
Its brain a thinking stomach
Its body a bag for tomorrow's blood
It rages across the radar
Blood lust in its Cambrian bile

A Kraken glimpsed in a half-lit dream

Grendel sated in underwater halls.

Basking Shark

The Basking Shark is a hundred miles of contented cow
The sea's blubbery combine harvester
Engulfing the stained glass meadows of her endless Elysian ocean

With jaws full of sweeping Baleen machinery
Intent only on her next gallon of living diamonds
She processes the Pacific like a saintly multi-national

The Basking Shark is the planet's largest sunbather
A Coney Island Matriarch
Washing her voluptuous cellulite
In the World's largest slipper bath

The Basking Shark is a hundred miles of Ambré Solaire
Smiling the Planet's largest smile
Her barnacled skin
Blissfully blistering
In the marvellous strapless sunrise
Of her awesome
Rippling reams
As she drifts on the heaving lilo

Of her blubbery plankton dreams.

Snails

Wandering homewards after Summer rain
I have often found Snails
Fully rigged on their silver seas
Leaving the ports of lamp-lit gardens
And I have stooped down
Like some fastidious Jain
Again
  and again
    and again
    and again
To plant them back in the comfort of gardens
Safe from the anvils of moon cracking thrushes
The churning wheels of brightly lit buses
And the crunching heels of unthinking lovers
Too busy fanning each others' ardour
And too busy smoothing each others' pain
To notice the shipwreck of chestnut Armadas
Wandering homeless after Summer rain.

Spider

The spider is spinning a rose window in the morning wind
An architect's blueprint for a Summer cathedral
Whose nave is lit by the warmth of the sun

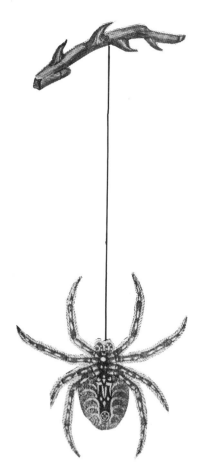

Swallows

Swallows compose Summer's elegy
As they decorate singing telegraph wires
With crotchety feathered cadenzas

They are leaving for Africa
A skein of Elgar
A flock of Greensleeves
Seeding Worcestershire in Ngorongoro

Upon their return
Something of Africa
Will bloom in the breasts of the Malverns
Then Bill Hedgebutts will write in to
Gardeners' Question Time
To ask what he can do
About Warthogs rooting up brassicas
Thompson's Gazelle nibbling window cake

And Elephants sitting in wheelbarrows.

Swansong Haiku

Autumn's outriders
Swans glide downstream
Escorting leaves to the masque of Winter.

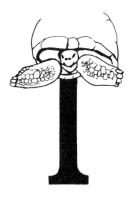

Galapagos Tortoises

The Giant Tortoises are making love
Like slowly excited buildings

They have been sending each other flowers
For over forty years
But only in the last forty months have they started
Gigantically courting
And shedding Churchillian tears

I like the look of her, said one tortoise in 1897
But he didn't get round to asking her out till
Nineteen hundred and eleven
By which time she'd found someone else
A brash Edwardian fast mover

It took him thirty years to woo her slowly back

And only now have they finally closed
The forty year, five yard gap.

U

The Unicorn

The Unicorn is imagination's ivory lance
At night she wanders the Uffizi Gallery
And leaps into the Primavera
Always on the tip of your mind
She is the Poem you have been trying to find
Hidden only by a lack of vision
Visible only to children
Who fill the World with unfettered minds
And walk into wardrobes
To dance with Lions

Sea Urchin

The Sea Urchin is a delicate mine
A globular, underwater porcupine
A hedgehog floating in a bathysphere
A snowflake rowing in a coral tear.

Vultures

Vultures are Africa's rag and bone men
Dustbin birds employed by houseproud nature
To vacuum the savannah clean of offal

With their Cockney neckerchiefs
And their bony smiles
They ride the hot whirlpools of African air
For hundreds of hopeful African miles
Gimlet eyes ghosting for ghastly gristle

Then,
Clumping down in their undertakers' robes
Like a squadron of intemperate flying toads
They squabble rudely by the meat kitchen door
Till the Lions can gorge themselves no more.

Three hours later the Zebra is clean as a whistle
And they are circling once again
A storm of leathery, foetid epistles
With their weather eyes cocked on the next main chance

Like Baron Von Richthofens hovering over France.

Whales

Whales are memories of the deep
        placid volcanoes
Calm chambers of light
Whales are blue echoes of our past
        Green cathedrals
Scarred myths in motion
And they are intelligent
Compassionate
And quietly spoken
As their flukes and fins assail the currents of the World
These great Sea Buddhas in lines unbroken
Curving down the earth as the dawn is woken

Until, that is, they are
                Harpooned
        to be converted into
                        ambergris
                        cat food
                        and shaving lotion
    oil lamps
    blubber
    and sexual potions
But then to some of us the idea that a Whale has
Any greater relevance
Is a pious ridiculous notion
For Whales are simply a product
To be blown out of the ocean
And they should never engage our emotions
Although we still swim with them in our wombs
And fly with them in our dreams

And some of us may remember that once
        long ago

It was *they* who helped us from the sea.

Blue Whale

The Blue Whale is the fading symbol of our failing blue Earth

The deep's great blue Buddha
The jewel in the lotus
Fashioned from fathoms of marbled blubber and sun
Our globe's vast   singing   echoing

om   mani   padme   hum

Our globe's numinous   paradise spouting
            umbrageous   Leviathan

                Forever fluke thrashing
                Forever sea grazing
Swallowing spiralling galaxies of squid light
Its brain as large as a thunder cloud
Its eyes as languid as limpid meteors
With a thousand and one shades of caerulean surf
Embedded in the saga of its keel and girth

The Blue Whale is the fading symphony of our failing blue Earth
Its frame as vast as an undersea church
Its songs sea psalms to its progenies' birth

But what in Heaven's name is it worth
This gentle, compassionate, fantastical ark
Floating down forty million years of fearless felicity?
            Well   seemingly
                Nothing
            Till the whalers came
            And the Cutty Sark
            The factory ships

                And the flensing dark

68

And yet the Blue Whale *is* the fading cymbal of our
Failing Blue Earth
And, as I gingerly touch its smiling contours
In the Natural History Museum
On a rainy day
All I know is that
Here
Large is   unbearably   unspeakably beautiful
            Like Everest swathed in fog
And all I know is that
Here, in this one   magical moment of
Awesome childlike contemplation
        All the achievements of mankind

Feel small as a mote of dust in the azure eyes of God.

X

Before the flood there were many X's of both sexes
Xephons and Xaviers
Xengons and Xuts
Xephers and Xengers
Xerods and......
Well, the list went on   As they do

But, someone at the Ark made a Kafkaesque error
And the X's were left to the rage of the weather
And Noah looked out from the poop of the Ark
To the part of the Alphabet left in the dark

Damn, said Noah
I've got A's and B's and U's and V's
I've got them all doubled to the nineteenth degree
But the X's are lost to the Gilgamesh foam
And the Alphabet's short of the X's we've known
The Xephods and Xaegars
Xagrabs and Xits
The Xentaurs and Xunicorns with the ivory bits

And Noah cursed on   as he did. But to no avail
As the Ark was tossed in the forty day gale

Until on the fortieth day the birds returned
The waters subsided
And the earth from the sea was once more divided.

Then a rainbow blazed over Mount Ararat
And a Bestiary poured from the Ark's wooden flaps
The J's and the P's
The Y's and the T's

The marvellous M's and ethereal G's
But, of the X's?

Only silence
And pages torn from the Bestial Ledger.

No more, said a somewhat shamefaced Noah
Will the X's give us such unbridled pleasure
I've just gone and ditched a planetary treasure

Shucks!

Then he went off with Ham to get heartily pissed
And the X's sank into colourful myth
A letter dropped from the Bestial tree

Such Xotic creatures
Lost in the sea.

(From an idea by Bilbo Dunion)

Yak

Rancid butter floating in well stewed tea
Is no great aid to the image of the Yak
Who would, I'm sure, prefer
To have chocolate made from her butter fat.

Yeti

Red haired
Splay footed
Sometimes glimpsed amongst the Frangipani
He lumbers on the edge of our imagination
Our shy snow cousin
So shy he barely exists
This gentle shepherd of snowdrifts
And herder of Yaks
Is he watching us behind our backs
Is he merely cut-price Zen
(A Koan for Western mountaineering men)?
Then again
Is he perhaps like the Snow Leopard
Can he drift invisibly amongst the prayer flagged stupas
Like a Guru from the springs of the Brahmaputra?
Or, is he always the lurching sky loner
Pummelling the thunder clouds of his chest
Breasting avalanches in his shaggy vest
Wreathed in incense and Buddhist charms
Ordering the weather with his Herculean arms?

Well, the truth is no one really knows
For no one has ever caught a Yeti
(Secretive as miserly John Paul Getty)
Or even brought one down with verbal confetti

But, before I go
And before he rises to guide you from
The Tibetan Book of the Dead
Try to picture him
Cloaked in red

The World's oddest, tallest, most elusive roof builder
Carrying the foaming sunrise in his tankard of frosted silver

Take Care! Zebras Crossing!

Be careful crossing the asphalt hide

Look both ways
For the Lion is coming
The rush hour road is choked with wild eyed Wildebeest

They have squashed many Zebras
Rolled them flat to make these crossings
So, tread carefully on the skin of Africa

Look both ways
Before you step into the seething savannah

Stand by the imposing Belisha Giraffes
Wait for the lollipop Gazelle with her sun on a pole

Take care
Follow the Rift Valley Code

If necessary seek the help of the tall Masai Policeman
With his uniform of ebony
And his pocket watch of Western wealth

Be Savannah certain

Look both ways
Be marvellously, patiently prudent
Till the Lion has passed in stealth
Or you may be   unwittingly

FLATTENED

By Zebras crossing yourself!

Zebu

A Brahmin bull
The Zebu is also untouchable
It is India's King of sacred beauty
Very heavy if slightly effete
It is the dewlapped Shiva that wanders the streets
Rising above the common herd
It is the alabaster herbivore
The four-legged bird
For birds take rides on its marble back
And beggars in tattered hessian sacks
Make way for these Gods who lumber past
(Whilst McDonalds executives look on aghast)
To drink from the sacred Brahmaputra
And dream under Siddhartha's crumbling stupa.

The Beautiful Alphabet

What were Tigers?   said the Child
They were muscled furnaces, said the Mother
They burned through Darjeeling
They had tails like a daisy chain of Bumble Bees
They had paws like the columns of Solomon's Temple
They had eyes like liquid daffodils
They were strong and gentle and arrogantly humble
And they weaved themselves through the weft of the Jungle.

And what were Elephants? said the Child
They were skin houses, said the Father
They had lovely hosepipes they waved at the Moon
They looked like your Uncle in a rumpled room
They had ears that flapped like sails in the rain
They had tusks that curved like prows of flame

And Dolphins? said the Child
They were sea-planes, said the Mother
Slipstreamed by time
They were Aquanauts hunting the Golden Fleece
They were sailing harbingers of surf smiling peace

And where have they gone? said the Child
They have buried themselves in our imagination
Said the Mother
And the Alphabet is chrome and steel
And the Plains are empty
And the seas are fields
For the World had no need of irrelevant things
Gossamer Condors with sun scraping wings
So, they put all the creatures in a chromium ark
And fired it into the star crusted evening
And now, on some far distant planet
The Tigers are burning
The Dolphins are flying with unbridled mirth

And the Elephants are waving their lovely hosepipes
At the sad and empty earth

Can we go there sometime, said the Child
And learn the Beautiful Alphabet?

Sometime, said the Mother and Father with tearful sighs
Then they switched out the light in their Daughter's eyes.

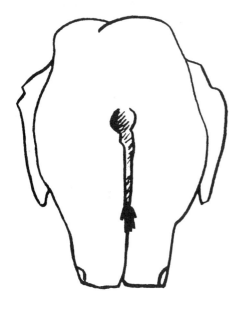

The Sad Tail of the Indian Elephant

The Asian elephant is a different species from the African elephant. With a population only one tenth of that of the African elephant, it is in great danger of extinction. Only 50-60,000 remain, of which 20-25,000 live in India.

A Sad Tail Of Poaching

Asian elephants are still being slaughtered in large numbers for their ivory tusks. Unlike the African species, only the male Asian elephant has tusks, which has led to a serious gender imbalance, with female elephants outnumbering males (by 200:1 in southern India). Male elephants with tusks have already become locally extinct in some places. Tuskless males (known as *makhnas*), which are usually ignored by poachers, are becoming more common. This unnatural selection is likely to change the Asian elephant into a species without tusks if it cannot be stopped. Of course it also makes it less likely that they will survive at all.

A Sad Tail Of Forest Destruction

The Asian elephant is a forest animal and its decline has followed that of the forests of Asia. Once it roamed freely from the Middle to the Far East. Now there are small populations spread from India to China, but they are isolated groups confined to the remaining fragments of forest.

The great forests which once covered the land have long gone – destroyed for timber, replaced by plantations growing cash crops for export, encroached upon by growing human populations for subsistence farming. Remaining elephant habitats are small, and shrinking under continuing pressure. Elephants have survived in national parks and other remaining forest areas, moving between them along their old routes for as long as they can. But many of these corridors are now broken or under imminent threat of destruction. Even if isolated communities of elephants survive the physical threats to their existence, without restoration of the forest corridors they are not numerous enough to be genetically viable.

A Sad Tail...with a Happy Ending?

If the elephants are to survive then land use strategies need to be radically changed. The present attempts to confine them to small reserves while continuing to treat other forest areas as timber mines and using most of the previously forested area for various kinds of intensive farming is unsustainable, both for the elephants and for the people. New elephant ranges need to be established, where elephants and other wildlife would have priority in management decisions, but human activities could continue. A diverse tropical forest can support elephants and humans. All the remaining areas of elephant habitat need to be re-connected by forest corridors.

Gaja Raksha (meaning 'Save the Elephant') is a network of environmental groups based in India, working to solve the problems faced by the Asian elephant.

Gaja Raksha (UK) is a project of Reforest the Earth. Its aims are to raise awareness of the plight of the Asian elephant and to raise money to support reforestation projects that will help ensure the survival of the elephants and their forests.

The largest remaining population of Asian elephants is in India. In south India there are surviving groups scattered in the forests of the Western Ghats mountains. Gaja Raksha is working with local groups on a study of the past and present elephant corridors and of methods of restoring and strengthening them. These groups are also working to raise awareness of the plight of the elephant and the measures which are needed to save them.

Thank you for the support you have already given to our projects by purchasing this book. If you would like to learn more about the Asian elephant or find out what you can do to help the campaign for their survival then contact:

Gaja Raksha (UK),
c/o Reforest the Earth,
The Greenhouse
48 Bethel Street
Norwich
Norfolk
NR2 1NR
Telephone (0603) 631007
Fax (0603) 666879

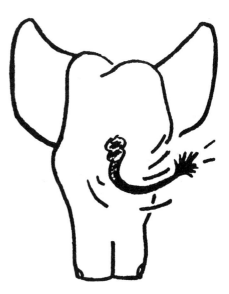

THE AUTHOR

Richard Bonfield was born in Leicester in 1959, but now lives in his adopted city, Norwich.

He has variously been a student, an Advertising Manager (for *Cover*, Norwich's first equivalent of *Time Out*), a satirical columnist, a bookshop worker, a CND Publicity Officer, the assistant manager of an off-licence, a wholefood worker and a caterer.

He is a committed vegetarian (although many of his friends have intimated that he should be a 'committed' vegetarian) and his poetry has now been published in a wide variety of magazines (see Acknowledgements). He is currently working on that difficult 'next' collection.

At home, Richard's hobbies include Zen Buddhism (on Wednesdays); Morris Minors (on Thursdays); a cat; and Addlestones cider. He also enjoys gourmet vegetarian cookery, Jackson Browne and a daily fix of Van Morrison (sad, but true)!